The Floorshow at the Mad Yak Café

Colin Will

Red Squirrel Press
(Scotland)

First published in the UK in 2010
by Red Squirrel Press (Scotland)
PO BOX 23896
Edinburgh
EH6 9AA

Red Squirrel Press (Head Office)
PO Box 219
Morpeth
NE61 9AU
www.redsquirrelpress.com

ISBN   978-1-906700-22-5

Printed by Martins the Printers
Sea View Works, Spittal
Berwick-upon-Tweed
TD15 1RS

Acknowledgements

Some of these poems first appeared in
Sketchbook, Envoi, Northwords Now, Poetry
Scotland, The Eildon Tree, Ambit and
Snakeskin.

The Suilven sequence was written on a writers
retreat in Glencanisp Lodge, Assynt. I am
grateful to Mandy Haggith and the Assynt
Foundation.

Contents

Entering your poem

First, a clean jump
from the poemside springboard.
You cleave the title's sunlit surface,
and hold breath against an inrush of adverbs.

Knifing under, you pull for air,
thrusting forward and up;
kicking hard at a resistant meter
you bubble through a raft of platitudes.

Clumps of 'souls' and 'hearts' float uneasily,
knots of 'pain' and 'lost loves' drift;
all the poem's dead leaves of old age,
and the adolescents' scummy bits,
aimlessly bob, waiting for the clean-up poet.

That's you, striking for the opposite shore,
where you reverse, and thrash again,
master of the 30-length stanza, Olympian,
spitting out excess '-ings' and articles.

Getting to the centre of things,
the known water of words,
the force of truth and meaning –
you have entered your poem.

The long walk in

Halfway along the path to the mountain
you expect a stream, and there it is,

rapid running at the end of a slow deep meander
where trout deliberate under the weedy bank.

This beat holds the brownies with a promise
of fly, and delivers on still warm days.

I watch them jig above the quiet surface,
little things with no intent, hard-wired

to live fast, die young . I'm getting close
to the base of the climb, where peat and water

join under wet sky. No trees, but stumps emerge
like bones of ancient monsters, and sawn ends

tell what brought them down. Felled for fires,
fodder, frames for shelters, sod-clad.

A cuckoo calls from a rusting fence, which guards
nothing but gorse and heather. A bare glen, deserted,

yet full of things that bustle, whistle, rustle, wrestle
with thoughts of getting up, never coming down.

Back in Assynt
to Jane

It's here again, that ridiculous mountain
I can't resist turning round to look at.
A double handful of sandcastle planked down
on a lumpy board of rock and water
and left to harden.

There's no signal here, I can't tell you
how it feels to return, how memories
dot the road North of Kessock Bridge.
I'd write it down, but the names
would get lost in the air between us.

The road swung round *here*
and we saw *this*, or *that*,
But description doesn't always help.
I'll just have to say the word
-*Suilven*-
you can picture it as well as I do.

The wind stirs up wee waves
on the lochan, heading East,
though the water's going nowhere.
Somewhere in the wet moss frogs
are fashioned from jelly babies
under a duvet of mist and drizzle.

In front of the Big House trees were grown
to frame this view – water,
bony ground, golden gorse,
scented shrubs, a greeting from the birches,
and the Great Wall of Assynt.

Now You See It

Today I find paw-tracks
on beach gravel, spraint on a boulder,
look round for an otter and see...
nothing... or everything but otter.

A family of buzzards
takes the morning lift
to work, rising early.

Each layer of sky moves
at a different pace. Air is compressed
approaching Suilven, driven up,
squeezing moisture into a new cloud
over Caisteal Liath, then downdrafted,
draping the summit with a fetching
off-the-shoulder pashmina of vapour.

A fence post at the opposite side
of the loch's water-mile dons a woolly hat
and moves away.
Brown blobs on a distant grass-flush
unfocus, possibly feeding deer
but more probably not.
We love to see patterns
in our landscapes –
imaginary lines, arcs, shielings , friends–
but perspectives can be false.

Two rocks in the water, seen
from one angle, form
a diver's silhouette, another
the inquisitive head of an otter
that's still not there either. Ask the buzzards:
they'll confirm there's nothing here
but the wind, circles in the air,
more weather flowing in.

Nor Any Drop

The loch's filling up,
changing the architecture
of offshore rocks.
A skyscraper's now a bungalow
and the suburbs submerged.

A break in the clouds
doesn't mean a break in the rain.
It sneaks round sideways
to fill the available spaces.

Now there's a net curtain of water
between me and the gorse,
softening yellow's brassy top notes
to a woodwind of cadmium.
The upper trunks of the pines
take a shine like varnished cedar.

Along the path, puddle becomes pool;
pools coalesce and start to flow;
path turns to streambed and from here
it's all downhill.
Suilven's gone into retreat
to rehearse the part of Roraima
in case the North-West goes tropical.

I pause on the swaying footbridge
to watch a raven dodging raindrops,
croaking at his echo on the crag.

Dampness settles in the joints,
giving me a good excuse to grumble
that writing poetry in Assynt
is no wet weather option.

I wake from a snooze and the mountain
shines in sunlight, as if to say,
"This is me since this morning."
Liar!

Making a Difference

The loch's surface pimples all over
with little circles, and then the diver pops up
in the middle of the commotion.
I speed clumsily upstairs for the camera,
stalk over the lawn in wet slippers
and keek round the corner
but the bird has gone.

A blackbird flies out from the trees
to the top of a rock, and its neighbour
stops grubbing in the grass to perch
on another rock. Eye to yellow eye
they hurl musical insults at each other
across a boundary I can't see,
like the one we always cheered
coming back from English holidays.

On Achmelvich's shell-sand and machair
we catalogue the fisherbirds:
a line of sawbill ducks; two red-throats;
a solitary tern, just arrived and missing
someone to scream to; a shag
looking for a rock
to hang out his tousled washing.

Between Loch Roe and its fresher sister
the sea flows upstream, quenching a waterfall,
until the moon's drag has passed,
and a peaty reflux refreshes the seaweeds.

From a high point we triangulate the skyline,
naming the jewels in the coronet of peaks,
Quinag, Glas Bheinn, Canisp, Suilven,
the two Culs, Stac Pollaidh.
Getting here we crossed an unmarked border,
dividing ordinary from Assynt.

Hide and Find

Suilven disappears again,
a darkness within cloud.
Swallows zip over the water
in the lea of the trees
where the mayfly
don't get blown away.

Bushes from the Himalaya
flash their pom-poms,
cheer-leading in shades
of pink and carmine.
The natives hide their little blues
and yellows under bushes,
amongst grass and heather.
As camouflage it's ineffective,
for who could hide the azure innocence
of milkwort? Who would want to?

The birch wood in Spring
smells like energy itself,
everything's shooting,
releasing the potent perfumes of growth.

A stonechat chitters on a gorse twig,
made nervous by an unseen cuckoo.
Below a grizzled crag I'm checked out
by a falcon, who can see
my inner pigeon.

The Crocodiles of Dundee

We leave the mud huts
and religious rituals in the capital,
pick up speed in the banking
and retail sector, zip along
beside the flying crosses
where a house once turned
and spit fire.

High above the first fourth estuary
our transport dodges
in and out of iron girders
freshly blooded in a twenty-year cycle
of blasting and protection.
Far below, sharks circle
for sacrifices thrown from ferries,
protein tolls for tankers
and the slug-like bodies
of underwater destroyers.

We stop now, glad of the rest
at Inverkeithing, its Gaudi Cathedral
speckled by salty drizzle. Then on
to Kirkcaldy, mainlining linoleum.
We barrel past Cupar,
the monument to Nickety Nackety,
and gather our strength at Leuchars,
where timid Jaguars race
through the undergrowth,
roar into the blessed air.

Now the silver brown Tay
heaves in sight, the last obstacle
on our pilgrimage, and formidable.
But should a people who took on Timex
be daunted? Never! We're close
to the surface, see the lines
of Langmuir circulation.

This might be where the salt-crocs lurk,
that zone between salt and brack.
Wind whips the tops off waves
but we can't peer through
the silty filter. The saurian hordes
are on depth sulk duty
and must await migration season
or the occasional gnus escaped
from Thomson's breeding pens.

Then our line bends, descends,
level with the waterfront,
the gleaming tesco, a discovery
in a hamlet once home
to Jutes and Jambos,
a desperate beginning for our Dan.
We'll remember this journey
for a very long time.

Thumper.

My pregnant neighbour came to the door
cradling her frightened little boy.
'There's a baby rabbit in our garden.
It's been injured by a cat;
can't walk; I think its eyes are out.'

I caught it in a plastic bag.
The hind legs couldn't kick.
Have you ever felt a rabbit kick?
Powerful.

I took it away, out of sight,
and swung the bag hard
against a wall.
From a torn corner blood leaked
but no more trembling.

I opened the wheelie-bin lid
and dropped it in. Only later
I remembered the visiting foxes.
I should have left it for them.
If I'd really been compassionate
I'd have left it for them.

Island Hopping

At journey's start, harbour porpoises
bow-ride the ship, a happy omen.
A speckled second-year gannet
keeps pace with the porthole. Far out,
a dark line of waves propagates,
but I can't see what's making it.

At some point, the vessel's track
crosses the line of the Simmer Dim.
At midnight the sky is lilac-violet,
the sea anthracite-blue. The sun
- an unseen golden presence -
glows the horizon's underclouds.

Berthed betimes at Lerwick, we stagger out,
too early for anything to move
except the Sunday wind, a constant threnody,
here whining in the lines of yachts
in the Small Boat Harbour.

The brightest colour here is yellow; but it's not
the gaudy cadmium of southern fields.
Marsh Marigolds flourish in the wetter flushes,
but patchily, their ore rationed, a rare aura.
The path to the Broch of Mousa
is a narrow track of sheep-flattened grass.
We step carefully, avoiding the little blue starns
of Spring Squill, as the sheep do. A bitter taste?
It goes untested – as if we'd eat sapphires!

Stenness beach is desolate, a ruined settlement,
memorial to the throes of Da Haaf, the harsh bind
of boats, swells, and shooting nets for fish. We arrive –
too late – at a gull's dining table, a clutter of crab,
limpet and sea urchin debris.

Every Sound crossing I search the waves
for that tall dorsal, orca's signature,
or the breach and blow of humpback or minke.
The guidebooks are definite – whales are seen here –
but not by me.

Off Noss, the sea is soupy with plankton, a feast
for sand-eels and pollacks. Tysties swim away
from our tour boat, red legs steering underwater
as their flipper-wings thrash. Disgruntled puffins
peer at the disturbance, then whirr off
to a quieter stretch. A lowered camera reveals
sea-squirts and dead men's fingers.
Nothing lives on the rubble-strewn seabed –
winter surges overwhelm, dislodge.

It's the same sparseness on the bald scoured land.
Unst's sour fell's peppered with alpines, a natural rockery
for the rarest chickweed, moss campion, and dumpy orchids.
Shetland is all nude landscapes, hillforms
resemble reclining bodies - bums, breasts, belly-button lochans.
Smooth slopes dip down to cliffs, where skuas and fulmars
swoop low, balance in air, gaining
a chill and whippy lift at the geo's edge
where vertigo enforces caution.

Road signs warn of otters crossing, and the bus shelter's a joke,
curtained in leopard-skin, with a chair, books, plant pots.
Good for a smile, as we swing south to board the ferry home.

Sealskin

I tread carefully on frozen puddles,
the nightingale floors of winter,
between the iron silences of rigid clay
and the stiff snaps of tall buff grasses.

Over the boulders there's a cool lagoon,
a basin where salt and earthy waters mix.
Here gulls clamour and the steady eiders paddle;
here swans pose, afloat on their reflections.

Where the fringes of beach and grassland touch
I find, in a stony hollow, not much of a corpse -
spotted leather, stiff, small, almost flat,
fur-patched skull, empty sockets, and still bristles.

I walk through the tight-wrapped town
to the leisure pool, scan the swimmers
at the deep end for a girl with grace
and eyes like frozen tears.

Exiles
(for W S Graham)

If you've nothing better to do today
let's swim in the malodorous waters
of the bay. Longshore drift
brings the biological flotsam in,
propels it in a wide arc past
Marazion point. A froth spit
spills vortices until the tide's churn
intercuts water and solids.

Here dark shapes patrol the plankton.
Sinuous tails propel the lumpen sacks
of bodies, the hoover mouths that strain
solids from water.

There's nothing White or Great
about these behemoths. Brownly they bask,
as barrels might bask, off the beach.

You and I, my whisky friend,
will doggy-paddle out to join them,
in our saggy woollen bathing suits,
distended crotches dragging
with the weight of seawater
and talent, caring nothing
for the fickle whims of taste
or the dorsal fins of critics.

The Jewel in the Gym

She comes here to chatter and pose,
tight leotard cut so deep we pretend not to stare
at the wide white gap between her small breasts.
Her skin dares the sun to darken it,
for she's an indoor being;
black hair, thin limbs, supple, twisting,
unstill.

I strain and push against mechanical resistance,
smile at her youthful lies, each a boast too far.

I tell myself it's just a generation friendship
but some days she drapes herself around my back
like a cloak with breasts,
and the weights press down on my heart.

Judging nature poetry

Typescript poems festoon the branches.
I walk through the grove,
letting blackbird's alarm
alert me to today's winner.

The whale's verse boomed and chirruped
on the constancy of krill and swimming;
why life is a fluke
and so hard to fathom.

To the beaver, all was willow,
and how sweet the bark of birch
in the deep clay dam of winter.

Doves sprang to the defence of wars,
for the multiple freedoms
loosed each successive armistice
from the pious hopes of peace.

A neighbour's cat praised
the stupidity of sparrows
and the playfulness of fieldmice,
and other victims.

The prize was reserved
for the eloquent silence of vegetables,
in which the wisdom of artichokes
brought forth a flowering
of edible metaphors.

Old campaigner

Returned from South Africa
crawling with angels,
the first affair, 1890's,
country picnics, stilted teas,
a hurried lifting of petticoats
behind the stables, button-fumbling.

Sand-blasted skulls, wreck victims,
poke through the dunes of Damaraland,
longshore breakers a constant cream line
on the browning beach, sun a given. Always.
Seasonal fogs drift inland,
tock-tocky beetles genuflect
to tip condensing drops mouthward.

Some time before the Great War
(around the Boxer Rising?)
in an ignition of petals
your portal opened
to my insistent knocking.

And now this evening,
viewing paintings,
I saw a likeness of a woman,
pictured you, many years ago.
That little tingle in the shorts
says the artist got it right.

Day Tripper

Today it's Ischia, blue water pools,
rectangular and cool at the foot
then hotter ascending, the top one
circular and 38°.

We wear yellow robes, drink limoncello –
as you have to – a lazy whitebait lunch,
and then a warming plunge.
It's just seawater heated by a volcano
we can't see, but it feels thicker,
like swimming uphill.

Water-wrinkled feet feel each grain of grit
in the concrete steps.

The tidal range is small by home standards,
so houses stop mere metres from the Med,
and the dark grey sand is soft, colourfast.

Some, more each year, die younger than I am,
and I sometimes think, not to dwell on, just
to wonder, how long? How many more
little tides will lap?

Across the bay, Naples sprawls
under Vesuvius' green slopes,
the long dark scar from 1944
less livid each passing year.

Singing, we return to Sorrento. The question
has no meaning: too many variables,
but some day it will blow.

After Fire

Not heat, not breathless heat alone;
not smoke, for that's just hot product;
not charring, blistering, glowing,
but fire itself, bright consumer, radiant destroyer,
strips us all to bare black essentials.

Who'd have thought the old man
would weigh so much? A plastic jar
that might elsewhere be full of sweets,
here contains the ball-mill's output,
white of bone mineral, charcoal the rest,
mingled to grey dust and millimetre grains.

When you park your car outside this place
you always sniff the air, don't you?
Just mothball outerwear, musty suits,
uncomfortable collars, constricting ties.
I could never wear black ones,
couldn't see the reason,
stuck to sober pink, dull blue,
or family tartan (can't go wrong).
No disrespect, but I have to be myself.

Facing the unseen fire, muffled rumbling gas jets,
I stare straight ahead. At least this time
I'm spared the sham of pretending to pray.
For what? I ask you. This is too final for fakery.
I remember his body, mouth open
as if in mid-snore, stubbly chin, no dentures.
I saw nothing else. There *was* nothing else.
I touched a cold hand; this time one
he couldn't pull back.

Behind the curtain the box descends
to the last conveyor. Volatiles vaporise
as the energy rises, molecules break apart,
gases ionise, a yellow glow in the flame's tip,
and all of it cloistered away from sight.
Nothing connects with the real here; it's all eulogy
and abstraction, but I know, deeply, Holst's Venus
was the right choice of music.

It's so different out East, but would the Burning Ghats
be better? Pouring on the ghee more personal? I don't know.
Could I watch? You'd have to. Imagine
the volume of human sediment flowing down
Mother Ganges to the Sunderbans, where tigers
lap silty mouthfuls, grit their teeth, roll back lips
to sniff the archaeology of pheromones
in the Flehmen response. That sounds right.
They blaze here, at the end of all rivers.

Caucasus pastoral
(By an imagined Vissarion Djugashvili)

In its cupped hand of peaks
the lake below displays the clouds.

Bees zoom over the scented meadow
hunting sweetness
and butterflies pursue their spiralling fights
into the oak's canopy.

My chiming sheep bleat softly
between bites of soft grass.

Around the evening fire
their eyes glow green.
My hound and I stalk the perimeter -
sniffing and sounding the night.
He is my eyes, and I an ear
alert to the wind of wolves.

We are our flock's teeth and terror;
their face against the howling world.

Bassenthwaite

Forty years ago,
shores of the lake,
sounds of a clarinet
waft over the water.

Blonde, ponytail, fringe,
green eyes, tall, poised,
in all respects
not the same as me.

I couldn't paint, as she did,
but I could blow a sunset,
duet with the reflecting hills,
improvise a freshet of waves

dancing on the surface,
a liquid serenade to the girl,
the trout jumping for mayfly;
their 'clop' sound like applause
for expanding ripples
and my shy performance.

Dissolution

The taps of rain on the plastic roof
become a rattle, a roar at times
when the larger drops hit
from the cloud's portfolio
of watery sizes.

Leaves tremble, twigs sway
and the whole bush
is blasted back in squally gusts.

The patio pools with water
too fast fallen to soak away
and in the loudest movement
of the storm's symphony,
paving slabs pimple
with short-lived hail.

Forced to close windows and door
I sit on the soft sofa,
face getting redder
as the pent heat climbs.

I hear you start the car,
listen to you waiting,
ignore the exasperated horn,
the gravel scatter as you drive away,
and still it's raining.

Don't

Whatever you were looking for,
it's gone. Reassurance was never on offer,
and I can't imagine you're really stuck
for a cup of sugar. I've moved on –
suggest you do the same.

I'm pissed off crying
over other people's spilt milk.
Have you forgotten last time?
The anger, tears, the revenge fuck
you took out on me, till we both stung
with pain, like iodine on a cut thumb.

Not again, my friend - the morning
after the afternoon following
the night before Christmas –
and this was in July. Granted,
you're a victim, but so am I,
so are we all; everyone in this
shit-sprinkled world suffers.

All right, you can come in
for an hour, a cup of tea –
no more whisky – a quiet
catch-up. But if you say
you love me that's the end.

(The first line is by W S Graham)

The Interpretation of Dreams

Floor spattered with insect bodies,
tan wing-cases, tan egg-cases the same shape
but translucent, glowing yellow eggs,
but we ignore all this. We brush past
a small table where a father and daughter
are eating, catching and sweeping off
a too-loose table cover as we go,
almost knocking the table over
with no apology, but no offence
is taken. We are, after all, in a hurry.

I could predict that that you wanted to interrupt
back a bit, to say that insect egg cases
don't look like that, but permit me
a little indulgence – this is my vision,
not yours.

We are joined in the interview room
by an interloper, who will not give way
(it's his office after all), not leave.
Two candidates enter together, confusing us.
They are husband and wife; they will not
be separated. I cannot decide who gets the job
but know it will be neither.

The fingernail roach shapes still lie still.
"Crunchy under your feet," John once said,
"after it's been fumigated."

Two collared doves depart in haste.

I need to hold on to this,
there's something here I need to know.

Field Notes

The ragged fox trots briskly along,
passing the gate of the field, spindles through
hawthorn staves, nettle cages, bramble traps,
emerges onto the plain of stubble.

Far side, among brightly bitten turnips,
winter-dirty sheep, shambling rooks, and,
in a glow of fiery feathers,
black head, red wattles,
cock pheasant scours the tufts of shoddy,
rakes below hardened turds.

All look up at the russet shadow
flickering dawn sun underneath the hedge.
The sheep, too far gone in lamb to care,
bleat acknowledgement
but the rooks rise in a harsh fluster.

Finally alarmed,
cock coughs and lifts off
in an explosion of wing,
an exhaust of barred plumes,
shuttles towards the paling moon.

Mr Self-Destruct does not want to workshop today

It's been interestingly difficult, or difficultly interesting,
but I want to go back to my room now for a smoke.

That wasn't a tear on my cheek, and I sniffed
because I have a cold, nothing more. What you heard

as a sob was an intake of breath as I woke from a snooze.
You were still talking, still reading the one about family,

about loss. Some constriction of the gizzard, a peristaltic
inversion, a kind of benign choke, wheezed free. All right?

What you said before, about everyone here having a secret holt,
the form of a leveret, an urban sett, was a rural writer's

fantasy figment. I escape to medication, that's what stops
the bees rattling in my shaken hive. What I want.

The Low Point
(after 'A Meditatioun in Wyntir', by William Dunbar,
c 1460 - c 1520)

"Dirk and drublie days" right enough,
but the heavens are not always sable –
some days there are true skies, and a wind
shifted from Siberia, to seek unfurnished skin.

Today the longer dark hours are filled
with entertainments then curtailed. It's hard
to imagine what true darkness meant
for plays, poems, music – summer pursuits all.

Scratching by candle, each scrivener wrought
on quires of deckled paper, by goosequill and gallol,
words of wisdom, terms of love and learning,
some meters of beauty to catch future's eye.

Warring motives lay on from every side.
Despair's the easy one now, so much bad news
in these cold times, suggest the one
begets the other. Patience dismissed,

and fortune damned – predestiny leaves no room
for innocent actions. We may as well be doomed
as blessed, and with an equal chance. Causality
is on a winter break, along with warmth and light.

Slyly, with some pretence of favour, chilly whispers
question why I carry forward a life that soon
I'll leave behind, with loves and friendships
broken links, unconnected leads and empty ears.

The forgetfulness of age is a brotherly service,
for remembrance of ourselves in youth
would give us pain – the way we were,
the things we did, the chances missed.

And death to come is final leveller;
low or high, we similarly stoop to enter
the same one-way system, a singularity,
the dimming doorway to a hall of nothing.

But yet, four minutes today, five tomorrow,
the nights imperceptibly shorten, and at some point
I'll know times have changed, that summer pleasures
lie ahead, and will return. The ball rolls round.

The To-Do List

I must get a fresh supply
of yellow Post-It notes.
The walls shimmer with them,
like the tree trunks in Mexico
smothered in a million motionless
Monarch butterflies.

I must begin my history
of the rice cake, its role
in dining down the ages,
its function as a tasteless platform
for nutrition, for flavour, neutral
for savouries and sweets alike.

I must arrange the flowers
in an alphabet of colour,
starting with the simple A's
of blues and yellows, grading
to the M's and N's of reds
and dusky oranges, finishing
with those complex consonants
of white, and white on white.

I must start to cut you
out of my life. I'll begin
with forgetfulness, those little acts
of careless negligence. Then the missed
invitations, random snubs, parties
where I seek the ones I know
you hate. Sooner or later
I'll introduce the closed door,
the unanswered knock, the separate wing.

Thin

We lie separately together,
not touching, in case a casual contact
leads to misunderstanding.

I know you no longer desire me.
You told me, after a bottle and a half
of good red wine. In the undesired

something shrivelled from that moment,
becoming bitter, certain, shallowing,
a leaf reduced to dried veins, fragile,

skeletal. And love was not enough
for resurrection. At the end of everything
the sweetness of bodies

was all, or the foundation
of all. Love no longer made
no longer mattered.

Spermsong

At body's being a bowl,
a crypt, cup to catch blessings,
showers, sanctity, clots
of chemical swimmers, lashers, lungers,
sucked in a cervical snouting,
brazen, acid-laved, muscle-churned,
chased and channelled, bound and blocked,
beaconed and beckoned, oviduct's aftershock,
peristaltic propulsion, goal an ovum,
fastened and fixed, membrane-mounted,
injecting a shot, nucleic missile
to merge and fuse in a spasm of strands,
old clock-starter, quickener,
blastula, gastrula, bedded, embedded,
between coming and becoming, planting,
placenting, a future what, a future who.

Erosion

I'd be grateful if you'd
dismantle me with some care.
A slow process would be best.
I'm thinking dissolution, but not
as in monasteries.

No black powder to be used
in my destruction please.
Plug and feather sounds
much nicer. Crack me
along my bedding planes
(you'll find them)
where resistance is least.

Chip me away gradually
like Michelangelo uncovering David
from his hiding place
in rude Carrara marble.

Constant dripping
wears away a stone
but I don't think
either of us
can wait that long.

Slice me as thin
as tender lamb
falling into the pitta's pouch,
and cover me with
the toppings of your choice.

Best of all, keep doing
what you're best at doing:
pluck holes in my self-esteem
until I'm Emmental `
without the cheese.

The Red-eye

I leave this at your ear for when you wake,
the shell I picked up last week from the beach.
You said you heard the long waves curl and break,
reminding you of times now out of reach.
I slip out of the room and close the door,
leaving your house as quietly as I came.
The parcels for the kids are on the floor –
just books, no toys, CDs or X-Box games.
I'll walk into town and catch the early bus.
My flight's at noon, so I'll have lots of time.
I hate goodbyes, you know I can't stand fussed
departures, tears we'd both regret, the pantomime
of hugs and hands stretched out for one last touch
where fingers fail but lips would be too much.

Petrichor
for Eleanor

Harsh cries from the trees, troll and ogre visions,
idylls, nightmares, signless tracks, waterbirds, frogs
pumping grunge for a zippy dragonfly.

The wind drops; sky is painted colourless;
woods fill with sudden mosquitoes
a nearby smoker's fumes don't dispel.

Sound of coalescing drops on plastic roof,
monoblocs darken. There must be a name
for the smell of first rain on warm stone.

Soil absorbs the early drops,
liquid films particles, begins to flow
through interstitial space.

Plant roots extend tentative hairs,
probe initial water, test its extent,
uncommitted, pending proof of shower's half-lfe.

Everybody says it's needed, s'been too long dry,
but there's a sense of something ending:
not summer, but sunny certainties.

Haiku sequence – China-Tibet, November 2007

brown grass
in Zizhuyan Park –
magpie's harsh cry

hint of snow to come
but still Great Dragon Wall
is manned by tourists

ranks of cracked pots –
a jigsaw army waits
in the yellow earth

frozen slush lines
the shore of Qinghai Lake –
waves not waves

chorus of snoring
on the Sky Train to Lhasa –
cold stars blaze outside

yak butter candles
send smoke to the heavens –
holy stink for our clothes

mother and son
beg from car to car
at Shanghai traffic lights

home again – leaf fall
allows light to strike
the garden Buddha

[Note on pronunciation: 'z' pronounced as 'ts'; 'zh' as 'j';
'q' as 'ch' as in church.]

A short history of Xi'an

The Great Walls of Chang'an once divided
outsider from insider, barbarian from citizen.

No more. We stroll along the broad rampart
between the parapets, peer down into smoggy city,

take grey photos with phones. A tall T'ang warrior
dawdles to the guardhouse, shiny breastplate

of moulded resin, helmet crowned with red nylon plumes.
In a side temple at the Great Goose Pagoda

I make three fearless bows to the Buddha. A little man
sidles in. looks both ways before kneeling.

He would have been all right, I believe, even if witnessed,
and he's surely better for performing right actions.

Some varieties of experience must be undertaken,
not just observed. In the evening the news comes

of a new feathered dinosaur from Lianing Province,
but this is not a novelty. That is how birds became.

Underground army

Emperor Qin lies under the yellow soil
suspended on a pool of flashing mercury.

To the East, where barbarians arise,
He is protected by ranks of broken pots,

sherds that no-one will glue together
for more than two millennia. It's a long time

to last, cracked and crushed in a pit,
with the fallen roof carbonised and crumbled.

Men grew trees above – Look! Roots! –
and aeons of rice were puddled and winnowed

over their fragmented heads. Ceramic armour is secure
against baking sun, the tears of rain and a history forgotten.

Where are the slain builders, the potters, the pit-diggers?
No trace, bones turned to crops, unmarked graves returned

to dust, names all lost save that of the dead tyrant,
here among His monumental crockery.

Credo
Kumbum Monastery, Ta'er Si, Qinghai

In the square, which isn't,
a row of eight bell-shaped stupas
and a single huge one,
reliquary and symbol
of Buddha-mind.

Light snow has fallen,
making it easier for pilgrims
to slide their woodblock mittens
forward on the polished cobbles,
around the shrine.

I marvel at the devotion
but can't share it. My way
along the Eightfold Path
is private, an inner thing.

So I stand in front of statues,
paintings, icons of compassion,
and make my bows. Always
an odd number – one, three, five.
I spin the big prayer wheels
clockwise, so the scriptures
they contain are read
the right way.

I leave small notes
in the offertory boxes
before each shrine.
I've come without yak butter
or the modern scented substitute
imported from India.
There's enough in the bowls
to keep the wicks burning,
the light shining on the monks'

reddened cheeks, red robes.
Tibetans' right sleeves are empty,
dangling, and I'm told
it's just a custom.
I want to know more
but I lack the language.

Within the largest temple
are this year's yak butter sculptures
of the Buddha, his guardians,
the temple builders.
Bright pigments decorate the images
in their refrigerated glass cases,
and I'm told how the hands
of the makers are ruined
by constant immersion
in freezing water.

I'm impressed but, as usual, baffled.
Faith, acceptance without evidence,
is not for me. Wisdom, hard-won,
must come to me from reason.
There is no third eye, the two I have
provide the proof of all there is,
and the inlook of Zen made the frames
through which my world is seen.

Still, as I laugh and smile for photos
with crop-haired nuns and their mums,
or exchange stares with nomad pilgrims
in smoky shrines hung with silks
and drowsy with deep bass chants,
I know how much we have in common here.
The continents and cultures
that divide us, don't divide us.

Om Mani Padme Hum

Iron Road to Lhasa

Leaving Golmud, we snake
through the slim passes
of the Burhan Budai Shan.
These ochre hills are plant-nude,
a dry land waiting for snow.

Gullies are empty, gravel-bottomed,
the few streams still night-frozen
although this high sun
will let them flow by noon.

Lammergeiers surf the thermals
alert for fresh bones of beasts
that didn't make it through
to the feather-grass pastures,
the steppe lands of Tanggula.

A grey-green carpet
knits the permafrost
in this undulant region;
haven for pika
and their hawkish neighbours,
home to gazelle, kiang
and square-faced sand fox.

The grassland is backdropped
by un-named snowpeaks
with grumbling glaciers.
Who would name them, who
would read the names?

At turquoise Lake Namtso,
just starting its annual freeze,
the last few bar-heads feed
in the silty shallows. Soon they'll soar
Himalaya-high, and glide
to the plains of India.

By an outflow river,
Brahmaputra tributary,
a wild bull yak stands,
furred for winter,
on an eroded moss bed.

Dusk descent into Amdo,
here and there mud-brick huts,
courtyards, yak-dung smoke,
little herds of goats and sheep,
dust devils from trail bikes,
flapping scripture flags.

Coming down, from the high spot
of the world, and half a world over,
pilgrimage season's started.

Next day we flow together,
a river of red robes
and tourists, clockwise,
round the Lhasa circuits,
as if to spin the city
like a prayer wheel.

Om Mani Padme Hum

The Floorshow at the Mad Yak Café

Food before entertainment
is the rule here. It's a taste
of Tibetan culture we're here to get
only we don't.

Cloudy barley beer is poured
into shot glasses, salted tea
with yak butter, a mild greasy drink,
into the cups. We sip quietly –
the Western way.

Then the long buffet –
Chinese dishes one side,
Tibetan the other.
Steamed buns with minced yak filling
are tasty, but not, I'm sure,
authentic nomad's dim sum.

In all the many haggis meals
I've downed, I've doubtless
eaten SHEEPS LUNGS, but seeing a bowl
so labelled and full of it, I skip
to the next tureen. Here
is SHEEP SAUSAGE,
a bland blood pudding.
YAK STEW is good, so too
SHEEP AND POTATO SOUP.
YAK YOGHURT
gets both my thumbs up, but not
YAK CHEESECAKE.
Dry grey cubes
of a crumbly substance
smell bad, and I can see
suspicious black hairs in it.
I'm grateful for a ubiquitous
Tsingtao beer.

Tables cleared, a buzzy sound system
crackles into life. A troupe
of relieved cooks and waitresses
do a shuffle called dance,
mime badly to songs
mostly in Chinese.
The costumes are bright,
might even be the real thing
but we can't judge.

On the other side of the room
a party of tourists from Japan
have had the same experience.
Two of them, I'm sure, are Zen monks
but I keep quiet. My Japanese
isn't good enough for conversation.
It's all, I suppose,
a matter of taste. This isn't Tibet
as Tibetans know it,
nor as we would wish
to see it.

Om Mani Padme Hum.

Last Rites

We have four ways
to dispose of the dead,
she tells me.

Sky burial is still number one,
even since the Liberation.
The body is stripped. All flesh
is filleted from the bones
by the rogyapas, the body-breakers.

Then bones are broken with hammers,
sledged to splinters and mixed with tsampa.
Only after the rock platform is cleared of that
is the next course served.

Call it guts, internal organs, offal,
heart, lungs, liver, brain,
the slippery bits, glistening gobbets,
mad bellows that used to suck thin air,
all the pumps and pipes, intestines,
shrivelled sex parts, tumours,
empty blood vessels, the silent tongue.

Last the muscle, meat, the griffon's favourite,
but these days a good hungry vulture
is hard to find. A potent medicine
used to relieve lameness in livestock,
gout in us, has poisoned the birds.

The fourth way is burial,
but ground deep enough to dig
is too valuable for corpses.
Only the minorities, I'm told
(with a significant glance),
choose this method.

Cremation is the third, but costly
in a land too high
for much wood to grow,
and as yet there are few
Western crematoria.

Water burial is an easy second.
It's a long way from these headwaters
to the estuaries and oceans
where the rivers end. Mekong,
Brahmaputra, Yangtze, all rise here
under different names,
carry their disintegrating cargos
south and east. That's why, she says,
we don't eat fish – maybe they're
our ancestors?

Maybe they are. What is a body
when no longer alive?
No sepulchre, we would have it;
but a lump, a thing of no further use.
What was us has left the building
to swim with the fishes
or soar with the circling birds.

Om Mani Padme Hum

Flights

Heaven is a deeper blue
at this altitude, above the fresh white paint
on old stones, this startling ziggurat
with red window frames. Look higher,
above the red palace, above
the topmost white one.
Just below the roof
on the front corner –
the sunny spot - a few rooms
with yellow curtains. That's where
the Dalai Lama lived.

Look higher, to the hill behind,
where a flagged path leads
to a meditation chapel
with a view over Lhasa
to the foothills of the Himalaya.

The summit of the hill
which frames the blinding Potala
is getting closer. We're merely
more than halfway to that height
the tabloids call The Death Zone,
but here I gasp and pause for breath.
My heart pounds and takes a long time
to settle before the next flight
on this staircase. The guide talks
about Red Hat and Yellow Hat sects,
but like the air it's too hard
to absorb. We're overtaken by the locals,
acclimatised since birth, seeking future merit
through prayer and pilgrimage. None wear hats.

We ascend the left-hand stairs,
come down on the right, breathe in
the view, descend behind the palace
to the bus park.

Turning at the roundabout
with the statues of two gold yaks, the road
leads to Norbulingka, the Summer Palace,
whence the last Dalai Lama fled to India.
We see his Western bathroom,
a giant radio stuffed with valves,
and in the moat outside, bar-headed geese.
One, on an island, rolls a November egg
laid in May. Soon the migration urge
will overcome the mothering one,
and she too will fly to India.

Outside the gates, at the market stalls,
I help a friend to buy a bowl. I'm rewarded
with smiles, a present of beads, handshakes
and hugs. I figure we've been ripped off,
but I don't mind.

Next morning we fly out,
a long take-off run, slow, slow climb, a glimpse
of snowpeaks to the South, a final view
of this blessed land.

Om Mani Padme Hum.